WORST of FRIENDS

Thomas Jefferson,
John Adams,
～ and the ～
TRUE STORY OF AN
AMERICAN FEUD

Suzanne
Tripp Jurmain

★ ★ ★

ILLUSTRATIONS BY

Larry Day

Dutton Children's Books
An imprint of Penguin Group (USA) Inc.

DUTTON CHILDREN'S BOOKS • *A division of Penguin Young Readers Group*

——————————— Published by the Penguin Group ———————————

Penguin Group (USA) Inc., 375 Hudson Street, New York, New York 10014, U.S.A. • Penguin Group (Canada), 90 Eglinton Avenue East, Suite 700, Toronto, Ontario, Canada M4P 2Y3 (a division of Pearson Penguin Canada Inc.) • Penguin Books Ltd, 80 Strand, London WC2R 0RL, England • Penguin Ireland, 25 St Stephen's Green, Dublin 2, Ireland (a division of Penguin Books Ltd) • Penguin Group (Australia), 250 Camberwell Road, Camberwell, Victoria 3124, Australia (a division of Pearson Australia Group Pty Ltd) • Penguin Books India Pvt Ltd, 11 Community Centre, Panchsheel Park, New Delhi—110 017, India • Penguin Group (NZ), 67 Apollo Drive, Rosedale, Auckland 0632, New Zealand (a division of Pearson New Zealand Ltd) • Penguin Books (South Africa) (Pty) Ltd, 24 Sturdee Avenue, Rosebank, Johannesburg 2196, South Africa • Penguin Books Ltd, Registered Offices: 80 Strand, London WC2R 0RL, England

CIP Data is available.

Designed by Jason Henry
Manufactured in China • First Edition
ISBN: 978-0-525-47903-1
1 3 5 7 9 10 8 6 4 2

★ ★ ★ ★ SELECTED BIBLIOGRAPHY ★ ★ ★ ★

Adams, Charles Francis. *Letters of Mrs. Adams, the Wife of John Adams.* 4th ed. Boston: Wilkins, Carter, 1848.

Allison, John Murray. *Adams and Jefferson: The Story of a Friendship.* Norman, OK: University of Oklahoma Press, 1966.

Anon. "Transcript: Former President George H.W. Bush's Comments at the Clinton Library Dedication," Thursday, Nov. 18, 2004. www. washingtonpost.com.

Boller, Paul F. Jr. *Presidential Anecdotes* (rev. ed). New York: Oxford University Press, 1966.

Callender, James. *The Prospect Before Us.* Vol II, pt. II. Richmond, VA: Jones for Pleasants & Fields, 1801.

Cappon, Lester, ed. *The Adams-Jefferson Letters: The Complete Correspondence Between Thomas Jefferson and Abigail and John Adams.* Vol. II 1812–1826. Chapel Hill, N.C: University of North Carolina Press, 1959.

Coren, Stanley. *The Pawprints of History: Dogs and the Course of Human Events.* New York: Simon & Schuster/Free Press, 2002.

Ellis, Joseph J. *American Sphinx: The Character of Thomas Jefferson.* New York: Random House, Vintage ed., 1998.

———. *Founding Brothers: The Revolutionary Generation.* New York: Alfred Knopf, 2001.

Ferling, *John. Adams vs. Jefferson: The Tumultuous Election of 1800.* New York: Oxford University Press, 2004.

———. *John Adams: A Life.* Knoxville, TN: University of Tennessee Press, 1992

Hirst, Francis W. *The Life and Letters of Thomas Jefferson.* New York: Macmillan, 1926.

McCullough, David. *John Adams.* New York: Simon & Schuster, 2001.

Mapp, Alf Jr. *Thomas Jefferson: Passionate Pilgrim—The Presidency, The Founding of the University, and the Private Battle.* Lanham, MD: Madison Books, 1991.

Mott, Frank L. *Jefferson and the Press.* Baton Rouge, LA: Louisiana State University Press, 1943.

Rosenberger, Francis C. *Jefferson Reader: A Treasury of Writings About Thomas Jefferson.* New York: Dutton, 1953.

Smith, Page. *John Adams.* 2 vols. Garden City, NY: Doubleday, 1962.

CAN PRESIDENTS BE PALS?

Not often. Now, it's true that Andrew Jackson thought President Martin Van Buren was absolutely tops, and George H. W. Bush called Bill Clinton a real "friend." But lots of presidents didn't think very much of each other. After all, President Truman once called Richard Nixon a "shifty-eyed . . . liar." Theodore Roosevelt said President McKinley "had the backbone of a chocolate éclair." And Andrew Jackson (who always had strong feelings) thought James Buchanan was such a big jerk, he wanted to make him ambassador to the North Pole.

Of course, some presidents just weren't very friendly types. People said that John Quincy Adams was "hard as a piece of granite and cold as a lump of ice." Nobody much liked Benjamin Harrison, either—possibly because he had a handshake "like a wilted petunia." Some presidents had wives as best friends. And bachelor James Buchanan spent most of his time at the White House paling around with a 170-pound Newfoundland dog named Lara. But thanks to history books, we know that two U.S. presidents turned out to be some of the best and worst friends ever. . . .

JOHN ADAMS AND THOMAS JEFFERSON
were the best of friends—even though they were completely different. John was fat and Tom was thin. Tom was tall and John was short. Tom was rich and John was not. John was fond of telling jokes. Tom liked to play the violin. And that was only the beginning.

Excitable John could talk for five hours straight without stopping. Quiet Tom sometimes didn't say "three sentences together" in public. They were as different as pickles and ice cream. But that didn't matter because Tom and John were best friends. They walked together. They talked together. And, of course, they took care of each other.

When Tom caught cold, John's wife, Abigail, worried about his sneezes.

And when John's daughter needed new corsets, Tom ran out and bought her some. Unfortunately, he wasn't sure what size would fit.

But, best of all, Tom and John had the same big, wonderful ideas about America. And whenever they had a chance to work for their country, they did it together.

ack in 1776 when British King George was trying to force the thirteen American colonies to obey harsh British laws and pay unfair British taxes, Tom and John got busy. Noisy John, who was one of America's best talkers, told Americans to kick out King George and make America an independent country.

Shy Tom, who was one of America's best writers, sat down and wrote the Declaration of Independence to tell King George the colonies were free. And together Tom and John helped make America a brand-new nation.

Then, when the new nation needed money to pay its bills and friends to help it fight off enemies, Tom and John sailed across the ocean to Europe and talked kings, merchants, and prime ministers into helping America. That was tough work. But they did it together.

And when British King George (who was still pretty mad at the friends for helping America become independent) rudely turned his back on them during a court ceremony, John Adams and Thomas Jefferson were insulted—TOGETHER.

So, naturally, you might think that Tom and John would always agree on everything about America—right?

WRONG!

Around 1790—after they both came back from Europe—something happened.

For the first time Tom and John had really different ideas about their country. And when it came to deciding how to run the brand-new United States government, the two best friends just couldn't agree.

John said the president should always be the country's biggest, strongest boss—because a really strong and powerful president could defend the country's laws and protect the people's freedom.

Tom said, No way! He told everybody that a really strong and powerful president might break the country's laws and take away the people's freedom. In fact, said Tom, an extra-superstrong and bossy president might even try to make himself a king!

And Tom wasn't going to let that happen. So he just had to fight against John's crazy ideas.

That upset John. Without a powerful president, John pointed out, the whole brand-new United States government might just fall apart. And John wasn't going to let that happen.

So, he just had to fight against Tom's crazy ideas.

Now, of course, John and Tom were very polite. They didn't hit each other or shout. But instead of walking out talking together they went their separate ways.

Soon, Tom told all the people he knew that John was "vain, suspicious, irritable, stubborn, and wrong."

And John told all the people he knew that Tom was "weak, confused, uninformed, and ignorant."

And, naturally, people took sides. By 1797, when John was elected to be the second president of the United States and Tom was elected vice president, lots of Americans had different thoughts about how to run the country. One group, the Republican Party, agreed with Tom's ideas. The other, the Federalist Party, agreed with John's.

YEA! John!

YEA, TOM!

YEA, TOM!

YEA! JOHN!

And the parties began to fight. Some Republicans and Federalists actually battled in the streets. Others crossed the road to keep from meeting. Everyone called each other names. The fighting even got so bad that John had to have a special guard posted in front of his house to protect him from crazy people who absolutely hated having John as president.

Poor John. He really wanted to be a good president, but there were so many problems. First, he had to find money to buy more ships for the navy. Then he had to keep the United States from going to war with France. And on top of all that, John had to move into the brand-new president's house in the brand-new capital city of Washington, D.C. But the paint and plaster in the White House weren't dry yet. And when Abigail hung her wash in one big empty room, it dripped.

Still, John's biggest problem was the Republicans, led by his old friend Vice President Tom. No matter what John said, or what he did, the Republicans were always criticizing, and saying that John was a "repulsive, gross fool." They even called John "His Rotundity," which was a fancy way of saying His Royal High Fattiness.

John hated that. And sometimes all the complaints and names and fighting made him so mad he just took off his wig and stomped on it.

So, in 1800, when Tom and John both ran for president, they tried very hard to beat each other. John urged the Federalists to make speeches, write articles, and hold picnics, parades, and barbecues to tell everyone that he would be a very good president. Tom urged the Republicans to make *more* speeches, write *more* articles, and hold *more* picnics, parades, and barbecues to tell everyone he would be a better president. And when, after the election, Tom won, John was not a good loser.

Instead of staying in Washington to congratulate Tom at the inauguration, John sneaked out of town on the 4:00 A.M. stagecoach, eight hours before his old friend was sworn in as president of the United States.

After that John didn't talk to Tom and Tom didn't talk to John.

John went home to his Massachusetts farmhouse. He built stone walls. He split rails. And sometimes he complained about the way Tom was running the country.

Tom went to live in the White House as president. And, of course, one of his biggest problems was the Federalists. No matter what Tom said or what he did, those Federalists were always there: complaining that Tom was a "scoundrel" who ate "fricasseed bullfrogs" and criticizing him for buying the state of Louisiana and a lot of other territory.

And when Tom, who liked studying science, filled up the White House with three hundred dusty old mammoth bones and said that real live mammoths might actually still live in the American West, the whole Federalist Party said he was doodle-brained and laughed like crazy.

ut Tom stayed calm and went on complaining about the Federalists. Finally, after two whole terms as president, Tom retired and went home to his Virginia mansion. His hair turned white. His joints got stiff. But Tom read his 6,707 books. He rode his horse, Old Eagle. And he organized snowball fights and running races for his twelve grandchildren. Sometimes he thought about the good old days when he and John had worked for American independence. Sometimes he must have missed his old best friend. And when an acquaintance asked about John Adams, Tom said that John was "honest" and "great."

John stayed in his Massachusetts farmhouse. His hands sometimes trembled and his eyesight grew dim. But he read his 3,200 books and wrote "Nonsense!" in the margins when he didn't agree with the author. He took long walks. He played with Abigail's new puppy, and he served pudding to his fourteen grandchildren. Sometimes he thought about the good old days. And sometimes he must have missed talking to his old friend, Tom. "I always loved Jefferson," John said.

Friends like Dr. Benjamin Rush, who signed the Declaration of
Independence along with Tom and John, said, for goodness sakes,
why don't you two make up?

Still John wouldn't do it.

Neither would Tom.

But somehow John must have kept thinking about his old best friend because on January 1, 1812, he picked up his pen. "Dear Sir," John wrote. "All of my Family . . . are well . . . I wish you . . . many happy New Years." He signed the letter. Then he mailed it to Thomas Jefferson and waited.

Would Jefferson write back?

One month later the postman brought a letter. John tore open the envelope. The letter was from Tom!

John answered right away. After eleven years there was so much to say, and Tom and John could hardly write letters fast enough.

When John's son, John Quincy Adams, was elected the sixth president of the United States, Tom sent congratulations.

When John was feeling silly, he made jokes. Once he signed a letter "J.A. In the 89(th) year of his age still too fat to last much longer."

And when Tom said they both ought to forget that their big fight

had ever happened, John was so happy. It was "the best letter . . . ever written," he said.

After all, John told Tom, "You . . . had as good a right to your opinion as I had to mine."

Yes, Tom said, people could have different ideas and still be friends.

So it was all right that sometimes John thought one way and Tom thought another. Little differences didn't matter because Tom and John were best friends. Sick or well, they kept on writing to each other.

And when Tom and John both died on the very same day, July 4, 1826—the fiftieth birthday of American independence—the whole country was sad, and people all over the United States stopped to remember them. They remembered that Thomas Jefferson and John Adams had been presidents and vice presidents and ambassadors and, sometimes, bitter enemies.

But most of all people remembered that Tom and John were best friends who had helped America grow up . . .

DUE